JOSEPH
THE LOST PRINCE OF ISRAEL

Copyright © 2021
All Rights Reserved Khai Yashua Press
First Edition ISBN: 978-1-7359069-4-2
No part of this publication may be reproduced, stored in any form whatsoever,
or transmitted in any form or by any means without prior written consent from
Khai Yashua Press

DEDICATION

This book is dedicated to YAHOWAH, YAHOSHUA and THE RUAKH HA' QODESH. In memory of our ancient Patriarch Joseph the son of Jacob. We encourage the youth of Israel to read and understand the words and story of Joseph.

TABLE OF CONTENTS

THE BEGINNING	7
COAT OF MANY COLORS	11
THE PLOT TO KILL JOSEPH	15
SOLD INTO EGYPT	21
COAT DIPPED IN BLOOD	22
THE EGYPTIAN WOMAN	24
JOSEPH CAST INTO PRISON	27
PRISONERS' DREAM	30
PHAROAH'S VISION	33
JOSEPH INTERPRETS THE DREAM	36
JOSEPH BECOMES KING	38
JOSEPH AND THE 10	40
THE 10 PUT INTO PRISON	42
THE BROTHERS GO HOME	44
BENJAMIN ARRIVES	48
THE CUP IS STOLEN	49
JOSEPH SHOWS HIMSELF	52
PATRIARCH GLOSSARY	54
PROPHESY OF YAHOSHUA IN THE 12 TRIBES	55

TABLE OF CONTENTS

NAMES CONTINUED	56
THE LEADING TRIBES	57
THE CURSED TRIBE	58
PICTURE REFERENCES	59
GALLERY	61
ABOUT THE AUTHOR	72
ABOUT THE ILLUSTRATOR	73

THE BEGINNING

I wonder… Can I ever be as strong as Judah? Joseph sat aimlessly on a rock during one very humid afternoon. My brothers are all great at something, but all I'm good at is herding sheep! Baby sheep walked about, cruising through the bush fields nibbling on any flower they came across. There was one in particular though, that caught Joseph by surprise. This baby lamb was very small, yet it behaved as one of the biggest rams! When it walked, it commanded respect from its fellow peers. As Joseph marveled at this, his head began to throb. "What a day," said Joseph. The sun beams down on all of us. Todah YAHOWAH for the power of his creation!

Hypnotized by the haze of heat, he was slow to realize that a jaguar pounced on a mother sheep! Frightened yet enraged, he charged at the beast full steam ahead. As he ran, he meditated on a passage that Jacob, his father read to him, which reads: **Blessed be YAHOWAH my strength, which teacheth my hands to war, and my fingers to fight!**

Psalms 144:1

Invigorated by the words of YAHOWAH, he recklessly dashed for the mother sheep's neck, to save it from the jaws of the jaguar. As Joseph ran, he slipped on a smooth rock and rolled his ankle...

"Ouch!" exclaimed Joseph. By this time the Jaguar noticed him, and charges as well, seeing him as a threat to his next meal. It's eye popping spots and razor-sharp teeth moved ever closer! "I'm finished," Joseph moaned. "YAH protect me!!!"

Out of nowhere a HUGE rock fell from the sky like a meteor and split the beast in two! As Joseph lay on the ground bracing for bites, he sees the remains of the jaguar.

He also sees the rock, as well as his older brother Judah, the fourth son of Jacob sprinting towards him shrieking a powerful scream. This scream was a warning to all other predators that it means death to mess with his father's sheep.

"You ok little one?" Judah asked, yet he lacked the slightest look of worry.

10

"How did you know I was here?" Joseph wondered, to which Judah replied that he didn't know. "I felt uneasy," Judah said. "Something told me to throw a rock as far as I can, then chase it down. I'm glad I did, or else you would've been lunch!"

"Todah Yahowah for guidance," Joseph said somberly. In his heart, he wished strongly to repay Yah in any way he could, but he lacked the speed and strength of his many brothers. Little did he know, his life and purpose would change very soon...

COAT OF MANY COLORS

"Are you alright, my son?! Here, sit and eat some bread with a little wine to calm your spirit and uneasy stomach." Jacob, the father of twelve mighty sons, was a powerful man himself, but he had a soft spot for Joseph, the son of his old age.

"Todah Father, but I'm just as strong as my brothers. If Judah hadn't been there, I would've destroyed that beast in the name of Yahowah!" "I'm sure you would my son. Come, me and your mother have something to show you…"

Sitting close by were Simeon, Dan, and Gad. These brothers hated Joseph with a strong passion! They wished he was never born because Jacob loved Joseph more than them.

"Do you have something to show us?" Gad snorted. "Why do I work so hard in the fields just to have Joseph tell you that I was slacking off?" Dan hated Joseph the most because whenever he was lazy or resting, Joseph would be there to give father a bad report.

"Don't pay any attention to them my son," Jacob uttered in Joseph's ear. "Come, for your mother awaits us with a handmade gift she made for you." As they walked away, Simeon and the others gave Joseph a scowl, as if he was an enemy trying to pick a fight. Instead of giving them more to feed on, he walked away peacefully to his mother's tent.

"Joseph! My son!" Rachel, the mother of Joseph was a quiet, calm, and reserved soul, but when it came to her son Joseph, she couldn't help but shout for joy!

"I heard you saved our sheep from a leopard today! I'm so proud of you! I made you a gift, something to remind you of Yah and us." Rachel made a splendid and vibrant coat of many colors that shimmered like gold. Israel and Rachel slipped Joseph into his new garment, and watched the dazzling sparkles go to and fro like the night stars.

"This coat reminds me of a dream I had mother! **Behold, the sun and the moon and the eleven stars made obeisance to me.**" Joseph's brothers heard this, sitting not too far away from them.

"The longer he speaks the more I want him gone." This was Simeon, the strongest of them all besides Judah. He hated Joseph and could not speak a kind word to him. In fact, many of his brothers couldn't speak kindly to him because of all the love that father gave him.

"Why does Joseph get all the love? Joseph never went to war, or killed a whole city of people with only two men! He never slew swarms of enemies from all sides just to protect his family!" Jacob and Joseph were belittling the achievements of the brothers.

Genesis 37:9

"Did Joseph ever protect Father's entire estate and household from hundreds of thousands of people in the span of a few days?! Now this little seventeen-year-old boy was saying he would rule over the strongest men on the face of the Earth.

"What is this dream that thou hast dreamed? Shall I and thy mother and thy brethren indeed come to bow down ourselves to thee to the earth?" The brothers were shocked and surprised to hear this rebuke come from father, yet they still hated Joseph for even attempting to lord himself over them.

THE PLOT TO KILL JOSEPH

"He needs to go as soon as possible," Gad stated plainly. Everyone agreed, save Issachar, Naphtali, and Reuben the oldest. They watched as Israel let Joseph run like the wind in the barley fields.

As Joseph ran, he sang praises, psalms, and hymns to YAHOWAH, our creator. As he was celebrating, his brothers were up to no good…

Genesis 37:10

"We're going to kill him." All of Israel's sons except Joseph were resting in a cave, escaping the midday heat. "We've got to deal with him or else our lives will be ruined!" Dan shouted.

"We will not and should not even think like this," Reuben retorted. "We must treat all our brethren equally." "That's not how father sees it!" Gad replied. "He cares for none of us, except Joseph!"

"Please my brothers! Joseph is family!" Naphtali, the middle child, was the fastest person in the whole world. He loved Joseph and cared for him. He wanted to save him, but he was heavily outnumbered.

"What would Yahowah do to us if we killed our own flesh and blood?!" Naphtali cried. Judah was listening to everyone's point of view about Joseph, and felt it was time to share his own. "I don't think we should kill him, but we should find him and throw him into one of these cisterns until we reach a formal conclusion."

All the brothers acknowledged the plan and seeked a way to lure Joseph to the cave. As the brothers conversed, they saw Joseph running towards them praising Yah, still jubilant from receiving the coat of many colors.

"Father sent me!" Joseph exclaimed. "Is all well with the flocks?" "Here comes the dreamer," Judah snorted. Without hesitation, Simeon and Dan sprinted after him and abducted Joseph from the fields of barley.

"What are you doing?? Ouch! Let go of my neck!" Joseph tried to fight and scream but he could not match the strength of his brother Simeon. They said nothing as they dragged Joseph to the pit inside the cave.

"Throw him in this large hole!" Dan shouted. Simeon tossed Joseph vigorously down the cavern, and Joseph hit rock bottom in no time. "Please don't leave me here! What will father say when he finds out about this?!"

"Nothing, because he will never know," Gad chuckled. The sinister look on his brothers" faces was all Joseph needed to know. He began praying earnestly for a way out of his predicament - any way out at that. All night he prayed as well, surviving the cold as well as the scorpions and snakes dwelling inside the pit. Meanwhile, his brethren at the surface, Reuben absent, were looking for a way to dispose of Joseph cleanly without leaving any trails.

"We should kill him, then cover his body with large stones." Simeon and Dan were fixed on taking the life of Joseph no matter what. "Instead of killing our brother, we"ll sell him to the Arabs for twenty pieces of silver," Judah responded. "This way we can get rid of him, without having blood on our hands. Then to fool father, we"ll kill a sheep, then dip Joseph's coat in the blood and say a wild beast ate him!" This suggestion pleased his brethren, and they made a pact to never reveal this thing to Jacob their father. Nevertheless, Simeon was livid! He wanted Joseph's blood spilled on the rocks so he could stomp it into the ground. YAHOWAH protected Joseph, and would soon grant his wish to be removed from the cave...

19

SOLD INTO EGYPT

"Wake up." A voice Joseph thought he recognized irked him out of his sleep. Rays of sunlight sparsely peppered the floor of the cave, with even less of it reaching the hole Joseph dwelt in. As Joseph began to stabilize, a thin rope was let down from the top of the hole. "HalleluYAH! My brothers have come back to take me home!" Maybe Joseph was still tired, because the only people at the cave were Midianite merchants, who purchased Joseph from his brothers for twenty pieces of silver.

"Let's buy shoes with the money, so we can trample the memory of Joseph forever!" Simeon shouted. Dan and a few others made a show of stomping their feet on the ground, as if they were stepping on a bug.

Chills ran through the spine of Joseph as he climbed the rope, reality setting in that he hadn't heard the familiar chattering voices of his older brethren. "YAHOWAH my Elohim, help me get back home to my father!" Joseph cried in his heart. His mind and feet weakened as he got closer to the top.

When he reached the top, the Midianites quickly seized him, bounding his hands together with the same rope he climbed out of the cave with. Joseph didn't scream. He didn't yell. All he did was weep. His soul was anguished on account of his brothers, and all he desired was to be returned to his father. Joseph cried bitterly as he was taken, yet he still glorified YAHOWAH his Elohim.

"YAH, you can return me to my father, I know you can!" He mourned and prayed the entire trip, as the Midianites made headway to Egypt.

COAT DIPPED IN BLOOD

Meanwhile, his brothers made their way back to Canaan with Joseph's coat dipped in the blood of a goat. "We found this on our way home, is this the coat of Joseph?" And Jacob knew it, and said, **"It is my son's coat; an evil beast hath devoured him; Joseph is without doubt rent in pieces."** Then he tore his clothes and mourned many days for his son, refusing to be comforted.

Genesis 37:33

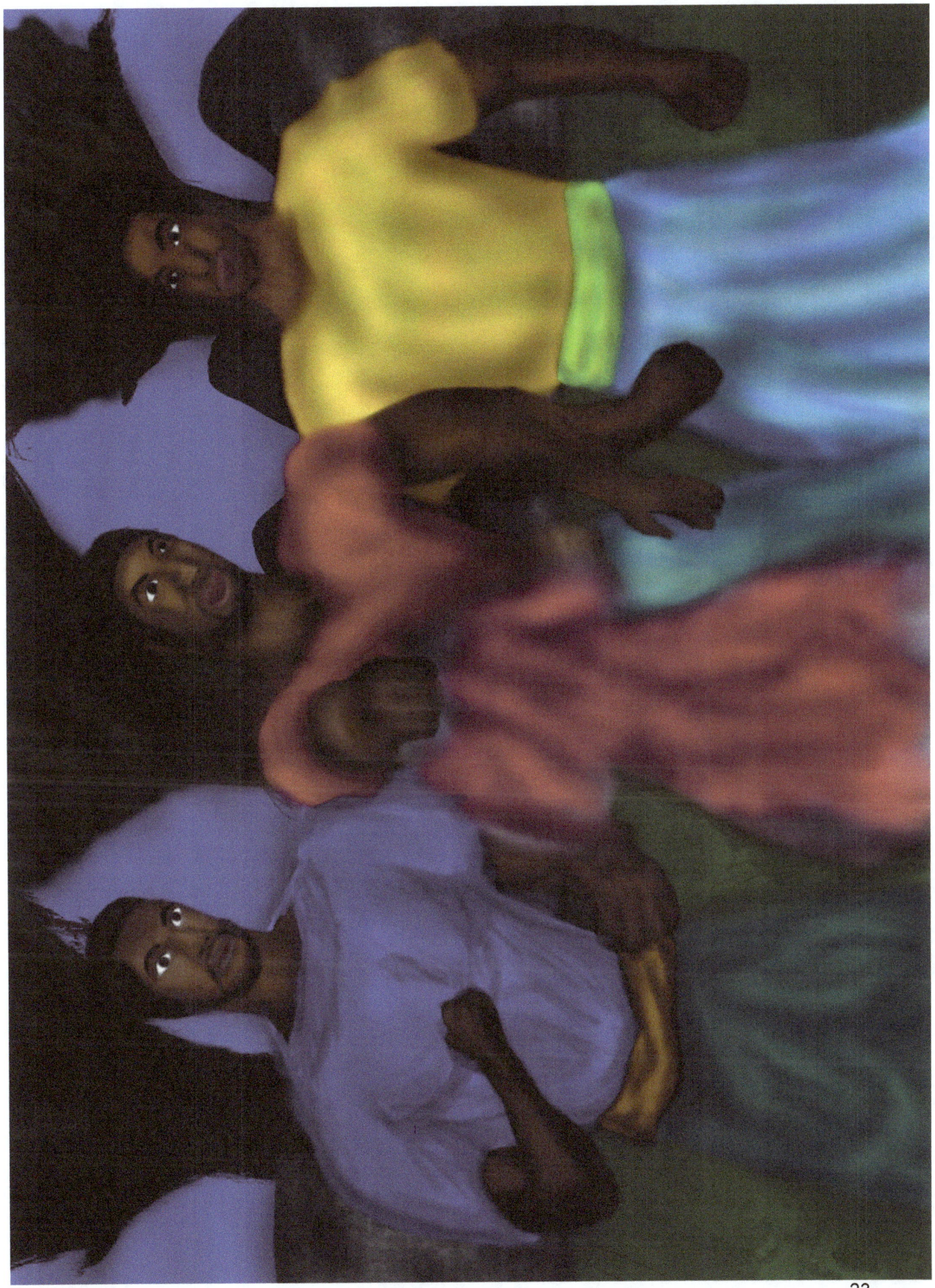

THE EGYPTIAN WOMAN

Joseph was sold to the left-hand man of Pharaoh; whose name was Potiphar. YAHOWAH was with Joseph. His master saw that YAHOWAH was with him, and that YAHOWAH made all that he did to prosper in his hand.

And Joseph found grace in his sight, and he served him: and he made him overseer over his house, and all that he had he put into his hand.

Genesis 39:3

*And it came to pass from the time that he had made him overseer in his house, and over all that he had, that Y*AHOWAH* blessed the Egyptian's house for Joseph's sake; and the blessing of Y*AHOWAH* was upon all that he had in the house, and in the field. And he left all that he had in Joseph's hand; and he knew not ought he had, save the bread which he did eat. And Joseph was a goodly person, and well favoured.* Potiphar had a wife whose name was Zuleika. She began to take notice of Joseph's hard work, as well as his handsomeness. Y*AHOWAH* made Joseph shine like the sun before the eyes of the Egyptians, because of his constant fasting.

He always put to memory the words of his father Jacob: "Don't let anyone take your crown my son." As Joseph worked and pleased his master Potiphar, Zuleika tried time and time again to seduce him. "Lie with me," she pleaded. But he refused, and said unto his master's wife, *"Behold, my master wotteth not what is with me in the house, and he hath committed all that he hath to my hand; There is none greater in this house than I; neither hath he kept back anything from me but thee, because thou art his wife."*

Genesis 39:5-6, 8-9

"**How then can I do this great wickedness, and sin against ELOHIM?**" Nonetheless, she came at Joseph every day to seduce him, but every day she failed. Day after day, week after week, she grew tired and lovesick.

One day, while her and Joseph were alone in the house, she caught Joseph by his clothes! "Lie with me!" Joseph ran from her, tearing his clothes in the process. Zuleika, seeing the ripped clothes in her hand, acted swiftly and screamed as loud as she could. When the guards heard it, they ran quickly into the house to aid her.

JOSEPH CAST IN PRISON

"**See, he hath brought in an Hebrew unto us to mock us; he came in unto me to lie with me, and I cried with a loud voice: And it came to pass, when he heard that I lifted up my voice and cried, that he left his garment with me, and fled, and got him out.**" She told this story to her husband Potiphar as well, which made him furious. He took Joseph and threw him in the King's prison for twelve years.

Genesis 39:9, 14-15

In the dungeon however, Joseph continued to praise and glorify YAHOWAH his Elohim for removing him from the temptations of that woman.

Joseph was faithful and trustworthy, so YAH allowed him to find favor in the eyes of the prison warden! **And the keeper of the prison committed to Joseph's hand all the prisoners that were in the prison.**

Genesis 39:22

And whatsoever they did there, he was the doer of it. The keeper of the prison looked not to anything that was under his hand; because Yahowah was with him, and that which he did, Yahowah made it to prosper.

PRISONERS' DREAMS

While Joseph took care of the prisoners one day, he noticed the King's butler and the King's baker were despondent that morning. "What troubles you?" Joseph asked politely. "We both dreamed dreams last night, but we don't know what they mean, or have anyone who can interpret them," they replied somberly. "I can, if it is Yahowah's will." Joseph responded. "What was your dream?"

The chief butler told his dream to Joseph. "In my dream, behold, a vine was before me; And in the vine were three branches: and it was as though it budded, and her blossoms shot forth; and the clusters thereof brought forth ripe grapes: and I took the grapes, and pressed them into Pharaoh's cup, and I gave the cup into Pharaoh's hand."

Genesis 39:22-23, 40:9-11

"This is a good dream my friend," Joseph said. "The three vines signify three days, and in three days Pharaoh the king will return you to the palace! Remember me though, when you become free.

"Show kindness to me and mention me to Pharaoh, so I may leave this prison as well. I was stolen from my homeland and sold as a slave to Egypt. Even now I've done nothing to deserve prison!" The baker, seeing that the butler got a favorable answer, began to tell Joseph his dream.

"I also was in my dream, and, behold, I had three white baskets on my head: And in the uppermost basket there was of all manner of bakemeats for Pharaoh; and the birds did eat them out of the basket upon my head." "The three baskets signify three days as well," said Joseph. "Yet within three days Pharaoh will cut your head off, and birds will eat your flesh…"

Perplexed, the baker sat down in thought. A few minutes passed, and he began to feel overwhelming despair and fear. Trembling, he laid his head down and slept.

Three days later was the King's birthday, and he held a great feast for his citizens and officers. Guards came and brought the butler and the baker out of prison. Pharaoh hanged the baker on a tree, and restored the butler to his previous position, just as Joseph interpreted.

Nevertheless, the butler did not remember the kindness of Joseph, but forgot him. Joseph remained in the prison two more years, until Pharaoh himself had a spine-chilling dream…

Genesis 40:16-17

PHARAOH'S VISION

"Bring me all the magicians and wise men of the country immediately!" The king bellowed. His spirit was troubled deeply because of the nightmare he had just dreamt. "What troubles you my king?" The butler asked. "Behold, there came up out of the river seven well favoured kine and fatfleshed; and they fed in a meadow. And, behold, seven other kine came up after them out of the river, ill favoured and leanfleshed; and stood by the other kine upon the brink of the river. And the ill favoured and leanfleshed kine did eat up the seven well favoured and fat kine." So Pharaoh awoke.

And he slept and dreamed the second time: and, behold, seven ears of corn came up upon one stalk, rank and good. And, behold, seven thin ears and blasted with the east wind sprung up after them. And the seven thin ears devoured the seven rank and full ears. The wise men and magicians arrived, but none of them could explain the dream to Pharaoh. Then, the chief butler remembered Joseph, and the dreams he interpreted.

Genesis 41:1-7

"I do remember my faults this day: Pharaoh was wroth with his servants, and put me in ward in the captain of the guard's house, both me and the chief baker: And we dreamed a dream in one night, I and he; we dreamed each man according to the interpretation of his dream. And there was there with us a young man, an Hebrew, servant to the captain of the guard; and we told him, and he interpreted to us our dreams!"

"Bring him here quickly!" The King commanded. "I wish to see if this Hebrew can tell me the meaning of this dream." The guards ran briskly to the dungeon and retrieved Joseph. "Where are we going?" Joseph questioned. "The great Pharaoh has summoned you," one of the guards said. "He had a dream, and none of his wise men can find the meaning. We have gotten word that you can reveal and interpret dreams."

Joseph's eyes brightened with hope and excitement. "Todah Yah!" Joseph shouted. "Yahowah has remembered his servant in his low estate and raised me from the depths of the prison!"

Genesis 41:9-12

JOSEPH INTERPRETS THE DREAM

The guards took Joseph and cleaned him, as well as shaved and clothed him with goodly clothes. Afterward, they brought Joseph to the presence of Pharaoh. "I have dreamed a dream," Pharaoh said. "None of my wisemen or magicians can explain the meaning to me," Pharaoh stated sternly.

"I have heard that you interpret and understand visions and dreams Hebrew," Pharaoh said. As Pharaoh spoke, he stared into the eyes of Joseph, looking for any kind of weakness. He found none. "It is not me who wisdom comes from Pharaoh, but from Yahowah," Joseph said. "Tell me your dream." "Seven good and fatty cows were grazing by the Nile. As they ate peaceably, seven horrible and sickly cows came and ate the good cows, yet remained as sickly as before."

As Pharaoh remembered the dream he began to tremble. "Is there more?" Joseph asked. "Yes, there is another," the King said. "Seven good ears of corn sprouted, lush and healthy," he explained.

"Then, seven horrible corns sprouted, scorched by the east wind, devoured the good ears." Joseph heard and prayed in his heart for wisdom from Yahowah. He explained the dream to Pharaoh in full. "Both dreams are one."

"Egypt will have seven years of plenty, full of abundance," explained Joseph. "Afterwards, seven years of horrible famine will follow, and the abundance will not be remembered…" As Joseph finished, Pharaoh and the wisemen were stunned!

JOSEPH BECOMES KING

"We must prepare!" Pharaoh boomed to his subjects. "What must we do to stay alive and not starve great Pharaoh?" The wise men inquired. "Ask Joseph, for I will make him commander, and second only to me!" Pharaoh commanded. "For who can find such a man as this? The Ruakh of Elohim resides on him; therefore, shall he be leader under me." Joseph heard and made a plan to save and store two fifths of the harvest. After the seven years pass, Egypt will have a surplus of food stored to survive the famine! Yahowah made Joseph second in command to Pharaoh in Egypt, to save the world from famine!

"Your new name shall be Tzapfnath Paneakh, and you shall rule the land under me." Pharaoh took the ring from his hand and put it on Joseph and put a gold chain on his neck. He clothed him in fine linen, as well as Asenath, the daughter of On. He was given the horse of Pharaoh and paraded through Egypt as the king's new right hand man! After twelve years in prison, Yahowah blessed him with the kingdom of Egypt in the palm of his hand!

Joseph had two sons by Asenath. Manasseh the firstborn, and Ephraim the youngest. Joseph gathered and stored food all the years of plenty, until the seven years ended. When the seven years of famine began, it affected the whole Earth, as well as the bellies of all the people. As word spread that Egypt had food, many made the long trip to buy food there.

JOSEPH AND THE 10

"What are y'all doing staring at each other?" Jacob shouted. "Our family is starving and all y'all do is sit. Now I've heard that there is corn in Egypt, so go down and buy some so we can stay alive," Jacob said. So, the brothers packed and took the trip to Egypt, save Benjamin. He was Joseph's younger brother, son of Rachel. Israel kept him close because he feared trouble would befall him as it did Joseph. Little did he know that Joseph was the governor of Egypt, missing him just as much!

When the brothers arrived, they bowed down to Joseph with their faces to the ground. None of them recognized Joseph, but Joseph indeed recognized them.

"We have come from the land of Canaan to buy corn," the brothers said. Joseph stared Simeon in the eyes and speaking to all of them he said: "You are spies, looking to find where our land is weak!" "Not so my lord!" Judah said as he rose from the ground, perplexed. "We are twelve sons of Israel, one is at home, and the other is no more."

Joseph continued to test them and spoke harshly to them. "As surely as Pharaoh lives, you are spies," he said. "Show not your face to me again unless you bring to me your youngest brother whom I have not seen."

THE 10 PUT IN PRISON

After he spoke this, he sent his guards to throw them in prison. "Surely this is happening to us because of how we treated Joseph our brother, who begged us to let him out of the cave," Judah said somberly.

Irritated, Reuben said, "Didn't I tell you not to sell the boy, and to return him to his father?"

Joseph was listening to them talk while standing outside their cell. Overhearing this conversation, Joseph went into his room and wept.

Joseph wanted to show himself to his brothers, but the time was not right. After three days of being bound in the prison house, Joseph let them free.

THE BROTHERS GO HOME

"Never show your face here again unless you bring to me your brother Benjamin," Joseph told them. "So, which one of you will stay in prison while the rest return to your father?" The brothers stammered and mumbled amongst each other until Joseph abruptly said, 'Take this one!" The one who Joseph picked, was none other than Simeon, the one who mercilessly assaulted Joseph and wanted him killed!

He was bound and dragged to prison before his brother's eyes. Afterward, he filled the bags of the others with all the food they could carry and sent them on their way home. "Don't come back unless you bring your brother Benjamin with you!" Joseph shouted after them while they rode off into the desert.

When the brothers returned home to their hungry households, they ripped open their sacks, eager to enjoy fresh corn. When the sacks were opened, the money that they used to pay for the corn spilled from the bag and onto the floor.

Children and mothers grabbed corn and ate and cooked, oblivious to the severity of the situation. "Why aren't you eating, father?" One of the little ones asked Judah. Petrified, he answered "Why is my money back in my sack?"

The other brothers looked puzzled, and opened theirs as well, just to see the same sight Judah saw. Everyone's money was back in their sacks, meaning they didn't pay for the food! "Woe to us!" Cried Gad. "This is only happening because we sold Joseph our brother!" Hearing this, Reuben muttered bitterly "Didn't I tell you not to sell him? None of you would listen!"

Indeed, they didn't listen, and now the dreams of Joseph continue to manifest and come true. Now when the famine grew stronger, the family began to run out of corn and foods. The brothers wanted to go to Egypt and get more food but couldn't because Jacob would not allow Benjamin to go with them. The time came to where Jacob said, "Go back to Egypt my sons, and buy us some more food." "We can't go unless we bring Benjamin with us," Judah said. "The governor strictly asked us to bring him."

"Why did you even tell him you had a brother?!" Jacob shouted. Jacob wanted so badly to keep his son safe, but he also knew that if he did not let him go, his children would starve. "He pressured us and pressed us, there was no choice!" Judah retorted.

Dan stepped to the front and said, "If we hadn't delayed, we would've been there and back twice already!" Judah caved into his sons and sent Benjamin off with his brothers to Egypt. He also sent a letter to Joseph, delivered by Judah, explaining why his brothers had come for food.

The brothers said bye to their families and began the long journey to Egypt. They also took double money, in order to return the silver left in their sacks. Meanwhile, Joseph awaited anxiously for their return. When the brothers arrive at the feet of Joseph, they bow to him, perfectly replicating his dream with the sheaves of wheat. When Joseph sees Benjamin the son of his own mother, he becomes overwhelmed with emotion. He ran inside an inner room and wept bitterly. Composing himself, he tells the servants: "Prepare food."

BENJAMIN ARRIVES

As the brothers approach the dining hall, they give their money to one of the servants saying, "This was accidentally put in our sacks and we wish to return it." "Don't worry, it's all right," the servant said. As if on cue, a guard brings out Simeon, and they rejoice together. They feast and drink together with Joseph, and talk. As their plates are served, Benjamin's portion is five times bigger than anyone elses!

The brothers marveled at this but kept silent. They ate and drank and were happy. When it was time for them to head home, Joseph had servants fill their sacks with as much food as they could carry. Yet again Joseph said, "Put their money back in their bags."

THE CUP IS STOLEN

This time though, Joseph secretly had his silver cup put into the bag of Benjamin's. This would give the impression that he stole the cup! As they left on the road, Joseph called them back, and said cunningly, "Bring those thieves back here, they have stolen my sacred cup!" The sons of Jacob were appalled and said, "Whoever is found with the cup will die, and we will become slaves!"

After the bags were dropped and opened, the cup was found in the bag belonging to Benjamin! "WOE TO US!" Reuben cried, for he had promised to bring the child home safely at the expense of his two sons! So back to Egypt they went, and all of them slapped Benjamin on the back of the head, thinking he had stolen the cup.

"What is this evil work you have worked against me?" Joseph snarled. "I was hospitable and kind to you, and this is what I get in return?!"

The brothers were motionless, not knowing what to say or if they should even say anything at all. Finally, Judah broke the silence and said "What shall we say unto my lord? what shall we speak? or how shall we clear ourselves? Yah hath found out the iniquity of thy servants." Joseph's goal was to test his brothers to see if they repented for selling him and planning to kill him.

He used Benjamin to test their repentance. If the brothers fought for him, praise Yahowah, but if not, he would take care of Benjamin and never reveal himself to them.

Joseph tested them by saying **"The man in whose hand the cup is found, he shall be my servant; and as for you, get you up in shalom unto your father."** This beckoned Judah to speak with him more. "If we come home and Benjamin is not with us, our father will die!" Judah said, his voice trembling with anger and sadness.

Genesis 44:17

"Let me take the place of the lad, and I will serve you with a cheerful heart and happy countenance; only let the boy go." His brothers beckoned Joseph exceedingly, and Joseph began to erupt with tears. "Everyone leave us!" he cried bitterly.

JOSEPH SHOWS HIMSELF

"I AM JOSEPH!" he shrieked through his tears. "Is father still living?" His brothers stood speechless in front of him, paralyzed and humbled at Joseph being alive! None could speak or utter a sound.

"Be not grieved, nor angry with yourselves, that ye sold me hither: for Elohim did send me before you to preserve life. For these two years hath the famine been in the land: and yet there are five years, in the which there shall neither be earing nor harvest.

"And Elohim sent me before you to preserve you a posterity in the earth, and to save your lives by a great deliverance. So now it was not you that sent me hither, but Elohim: and he hath made me a father to Pharaoh, and lord of all his house, and a ruler throughout all the land of Egypt."

Genesis 45:5-8

"Go quickly, our father is waiting for us!" Joseph exclaimed. So, the brothers went and returned with everything they owned, settling in the land of Goshen. Pharaoh allowed Joseph to set aside the best portion of land for his family. "Now i am ready to die, because I have seen the face of my son Joseph at last!" Jacob was an old man full of years, but at this moment it was as if fifty years fell off his shoulders! He embraced his son, face gleaming, and thanked YAHOWAH for preserving the life and dignity of his son Joseph.

PATRIARCH GLOSSARY

TWELVE TRIBES IN REVELATIONS 7

JUDAH (H3063) - Praise

REUBEN (H7205) - Behold the son

GAD (H1410) - To overcome/Troop

ASHER (H836) - Happy/blessed

NAPHTALI (H5321) - to wrestle with

MANASSEH (H4519) - To forget

SIMEON (H8095) - Hearing and obeying

LEVI (H3878) - Joined

ISSACHAR (H3485) - Reward

ZEBULUN (H2074) - Habitation/dwelling place

JOSEPH (H3130) - He will add

BENJAMIN (H1144) - Son of the right hand

PROPHESY OF YAHOSHUA IN THE 12 TRIBES

The Hebrew names of the tribes tell a poetic story when you remember that YAHOSHUA is the volume of the book (Psalms 40:7, Hebrews 10:7). The story revealed is...

Behold the son (YAHOSHUA) of Judah has overcome. He is blessed! He strove against forgetfulness and he has heard Levi. He is rewarded with a dwelling place. He is added to the right hand of YAH!

When we consider that YAHOSHUA is the word, we can understand the deeper hebraic meaning of the names. When THE RUAKH HA' QODESH led Jacob into naming his children, it was to give glory to the Son of YAH, who is YAHOSHUA.

NAMES CONTINUED

DAN (H1777) - To Judge.

JACOB (H3290) - Supplanter

LEAH (H3812) - Weary

RACHEL (H7353) - A female sheep

EPHRAIM (H669) - Double fruit

THE LEADING TRIBES

The 12 Patriarchs are the sons of Jacob. Each son had children, and began to multiply exceedingly. YAHOWAH blessed each individual tribe, but assigned a select few to specific roles.

The first role is the kingship, which belongs to the tribe of Judah. This tribe rules over the other tribes, and leads them out into battle. The next role is the Priestood, which belongs to Levi. Priests are responsible for leading the nation spiritually. They offer sacrifices to YAHOWAH, and teach the people the law, statues, and commandments. The last role is the double portion. This gift was given to Joseph, which means that he inherited two tribes. These tribes were Manasseh and Ephriam, his two sons.

Originally, these three gifts belonged to Reuben the first born. YAHOWAH took away all of his gifts because he defiled his fathers bed (Genesis 35:22). Reuben's gifts are now distributed between three tribes.

THE CURSED TRIBE

The tribe of Dan is the least of all the tribes, and was cursed by YAH for his hatred of Joseph. Dan's curse in Genesis 49 was to be a serpent by the way. He was prophesied to be a serpent that bites the heel of the horse, so that the rider falls backward. "The way" represents YAHOSHUA, as mentioned in John 14:6 (I am the way the truth and the life.) The serpent represents the devil, who stands in the way of us and YAHOSHUA Himself. The way also represents the only path in which we can be saved, which is YAHOSHUA.

In the testament of Dan 7:3, we see Dan prophesying that his tribe and kindred would fall away and become alienated from the rest of the tribes. This prophesy is for Judas Iscariot. This man was from the tribe of Dan (The Geneologies of the Twelve Apostles verse 10), and stood in the way of YAHOSHUA by selling him out to the Chief Priests. Judas was a man from Dan who bit the Messiah in the heel; thus fulfilling his prophesy, and condeming his soul.

PICTURE REFERENCES

PICTURE 1 - Genesis 39:19

PICTURE 2 - Genesis 41:45

PICTURE 3 - Genesis 37:31

PICTURE 4 - Genesis 37:3

PICTURE 5 - Genesis 41:42

PICTURE 6 - Genesis 42:27

PICTURE 7 - Genesis 42:9

PICTURE 8 - Genesis 37:23

PICTURE 9 - Genesis 39:12

PICTURE 10 - Genesis 37:4

PICTURE 11 - Genesis 41:15-16

PICTURE 12 - Genesis 37:24

PICTURE 13 - Genesis 40:9-11

PICTURE 14 - Genesis 41:14

PICTURE 15 - Genesis 39:1

PICTURE 16 - Genesis 39:3

PICTURE 17 - Jasher 53:18-23

PICTURE 18 - Jasher 41:5

PICTURE 19 - Testament of Judah 2:1-7

PICTURE 20 - Genesis 37:3

PICTURE 21 - Genesis 46:29

GALLERY

4

9

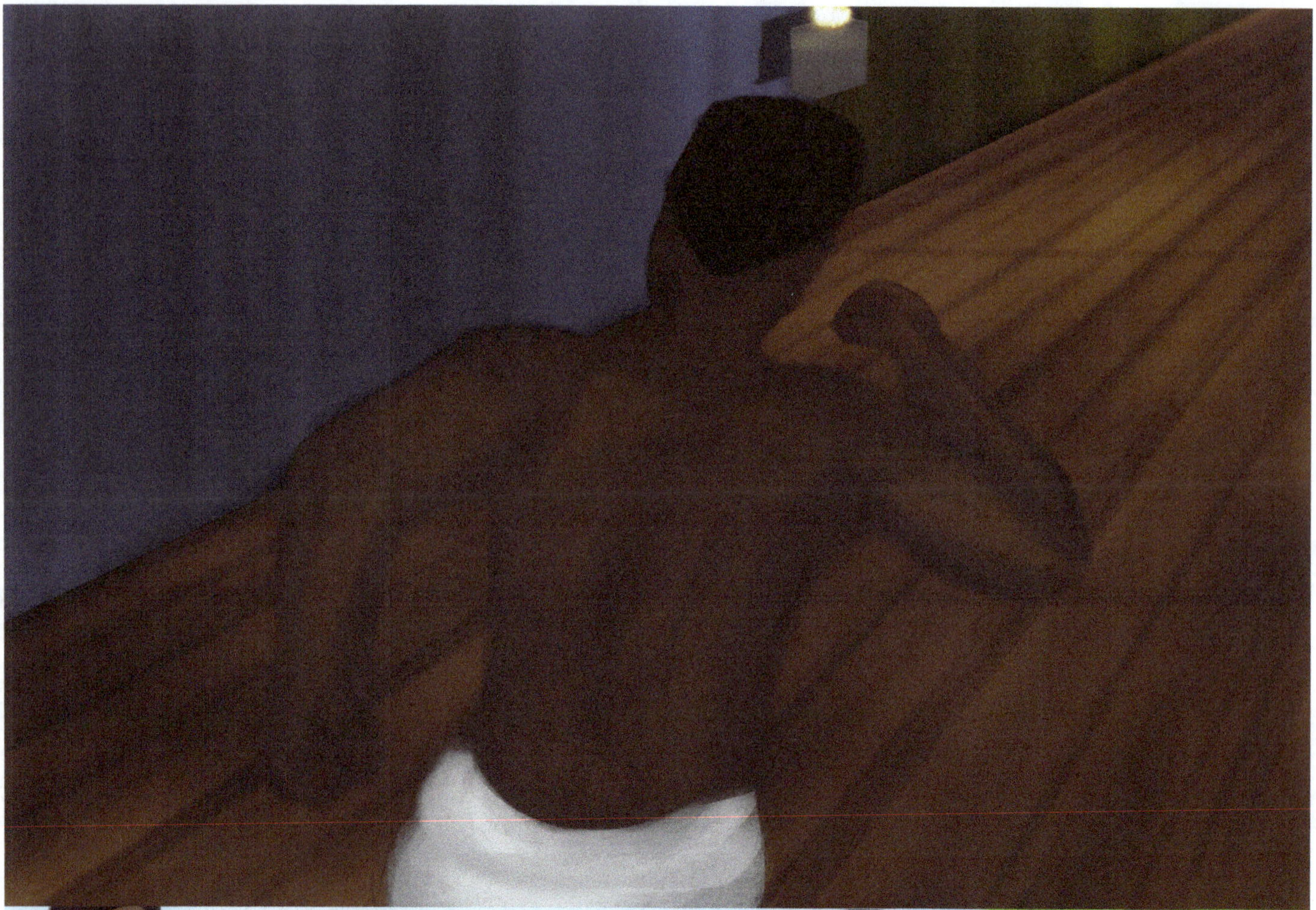

10

64

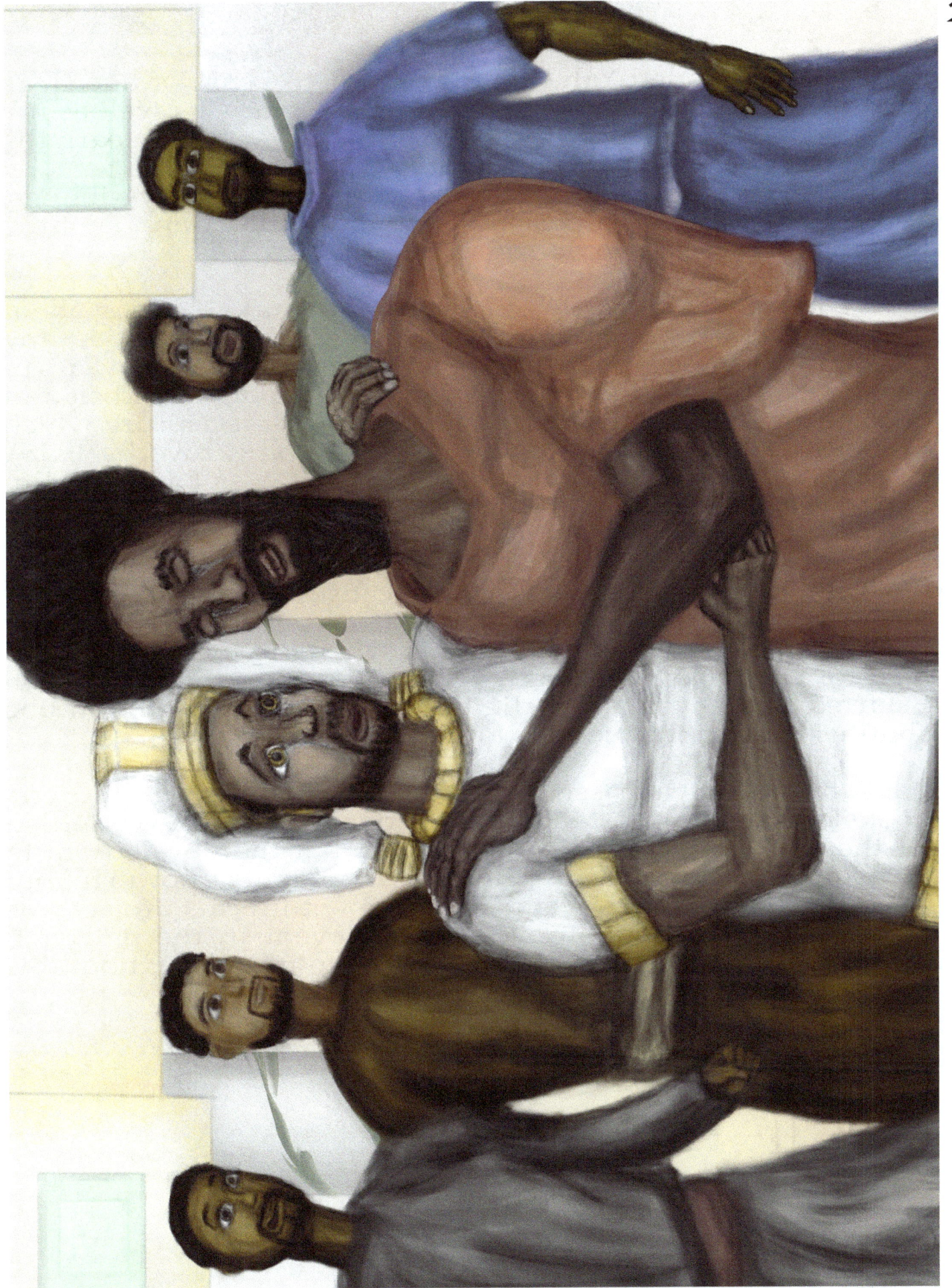

ABOUT THE ILLUSTRATOR

My name is JediYah Melek II, I am 13 years of age. This is my background of how I came into the truth, as well as my inspiration for this book. I was born into this walk to learn the way, truth and the life of our savior YAHOSHUA HA' MASHIAKH, by my father, JediYah Melek. I am the youngest out of my siblings, and I've always had a passion for making illustrations of the visualizations that I could see in my mind.

When I was a lot younger I would make comics about how YAHOWAH hears prayers. However, I soon forgot about my passion when I became a little older at around 10 or 11 years of age. I was pretty confused about my gifts and I would sit and do nothing all day. I remember I had found a scripture which brought me to where I was supposed to be (Proverbs 19:15). YAHOWAH used this opportunity to lift my eyes back on Him and to serve Him with all my heart in the form of artwork.

It started with drawing artwork from the Ethiopian Hebrew illustrations. I was reluctant at first because I'd never specialized in drawing people. It was a slow and very steady process but I kept getting better and better. Later when I turned 12, I got an iPad for my artwork. It was a very new thing for me, but soon I started to do everything digitally. I created a small Youtube channel to keep the memory of the drawings.

A month or two passed and we agreed on making children's books based on important bible lessons for youths. We settled on the 12 tribes and their testimonies, but that leveled out to focusing on Joseph because his story is the most powerful out of all his brothers. My overall purpose within this project was to bring to visualization every major event in the patriarch Joseph's life. YAHOWAH was always true to me throughout this entire process!

Shalom,

JediYah II

JediYah Melek II

www.ingramcontent.com/pod-product-compliance
Lightning Source LLC
Chambersburg PA
CBHW081421080526
44589CB00016B/2618